The Colophon's Best Vegetarian Recipes

by
Ray Dunn
and
Taimi Dunn Gorman

COLOPHON: (kol 'e fon')
1. A publisher's distinctive emblem.
2. An inscription at the end of a book, usually with facts relative to its publication.
3. Greek koloph'on: summit, finishing touch, the last word.
    (pronounced "Call- a-fawn" Cafe)

MAMA COLOPHON
(our founder)

Published by
Mama Colophon Inc.
1208 11th St
Bellingham, Washington, 98225
(360) 647-0092

A big thank you to all Colophon staff, past and present, who contributed their culinary knowledge and special recipes to the Colophon Cafe.
Thanks also to our many customers around the world, whose thoughtful comments and appreciative palates made this book possible!

MAMA COLOPHON
(our founder)

"Nowhere can I think so happily as in a train...I see a cow, and I wonder what it is like to be a cow, and I wonder whether the cow wonders what it is like to be me."

-A.A. Milne

Best Vegetarian Recipes
of The Colophon Cafe
Introduction

When we set out to do a vegetarian cookbook, we had do to some research. There are many types of vegetarians. Some do not eat any animal products, and others include dairy or seafood into their diets. The Colophon Cafe developed part of its fame by offering vegetarian dishes that would suit almost everyone.

After some discussion, we decided that some recipes using dairy products would be accepted for this book. We hope we've chosen foods most people will be happy to fix for their families and friends, and we've tried to make them as easy as possible to prepare and still maintain their excellence.

The new Vegetarian Diet Pyramid recommends including whole fruits, vegetables, grains and legumes at each meal. Nuts, seeds, egg whites, soy milk, dairy products and plant oils are recommended daily. Egg yolks and sweets may be included occasionally. We've tried to include most of these healthy foods in our dishes to help you plan meals.

The recipes were collected from items we serve already, favorites of our staff and friends and generally anything we love to cook. Ray Dunn's influence is big in this book because of his travels to exotic locales and the cooking he's experienced all over the world.

We hope you will enjoy this book! Happy dining!

"Paradise is where I am."
Voltaire, 1694-1774

Best Vegetarian Recipes

Contents

Alphabetical Index
on page 80

Appetizers

Soups

Salads

Side Dishes

Entrees

Desserts

Appetizers

"He who comes first, eats first."
Eike von Repkow, 1219-1233,
Sachsenspiegel

Galloping Guacamole

Numerous trips to Mexico have only increased our fondness for this traditional dish.

Take the outer peel off the avocados, remove pits. Mash them with the back of a fork.

Remove the seed from the chilies before you chop them unless you want a full gallop.

Stir in chilies, onion, lime juice, cumin, chili powder and salt.

If you are not serving the guacamole right away cover it tightly with clear wrap, pushing the wrap lightly onto the mixture to keep it from turning dark.

Use the green leafy stuff to line a platter or bowl with the guacamole in the center.

2 large avocados
   or 4 small ones

1/2 red onion, diced
1 teaspoon cumin
1 teaspoon chili powder
1 or 2 finely chopped
   canned whole green
   chilies
2 Tablespoons lime juice
1 teaspoon salt

some green leafy stuff like
   lettuce

Serve with tortilla chips and a good Mexican Beer.

Serves 4

Spicy
Quesadillas

Quesadilla quarters make yummy appetizers, especially
with guacamole and salsa.
The spicy Jack cheese and chili powder give these a bite.

Pour one tablespoon oil in the bottom of a sauce pan and heat to medium. Cook onion in oil until soft. Stir in cumin, chili powder and refried beans until mixture is hot.

3 Tablespoons olive oil
1 medium onion, chopped
3/4 teaspoon cumin
1 teaspoon chili powder
1 cup vegetarian refried beans

Heat 2 tablespoons olive oil in skillet. Add one tortilla and cook 30 seconds. Turn over. Evenly spread half the bean mixture from sauce pan and half the cheese onto one tortilla. Top with second tortilla and flip over on pan. Cook until brown. Repeat with remaining tortillas.

4 flour tortillas

1 1/2 cups hot pepper Jack cheese, grated

Cut into quarters for serving.

Top with dab of guacamole.

Makes 8 quarter pieces
Serves four as an appetizer

3

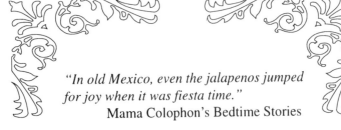

"In old Mexico, even the jalapenos jumped for joy when it was fiesta time."
Mama Colophon's Bedtime Stories

MAMA COLOPHON
(our founder)

Jumping Jalapenos

Party food of the most colorful kind.

Cut peppers in half length-wise; remove seeds. Combine cheeses, spoon evenly into pepper halves.

Place halves in a 13 "x 9" x 2" inch baking dish coated with cooking spray. Bake uncovered at 350° for 30 minutes or until bubbly and lightly browned.

Serve warm with salsa and beer.

12 large, fresh jalapenos
1/2 cup nonfat cream cheese, softened
1/4 cup shredded mozzarella
1/4 cup grated parmesan cheese
vegetable cooking spray
salsa

Makes twenty four

5

Chili Relleno Cheese Bars

Another fast recipe that makes the house smell great as it cooks.

Preheat oven to 400 degrees. Spray 8 inch square pan with vegetable oil spray. Beat the eggs in a mixing bowl until smooth. Gradually add cottage cheese, flour and baking powder. Beat until smooth.

Stir in chilies and the next three ingredients. Pour into pan. Bake uncovered at 400" for 15 minutes; reduce heat to 350" and bake for 35 more minutes or until firm. Let stand 15 minutes. Cut into 12 bars. Serve warm with salsa.

4 eggs
1 cup cottage cheese
1/4 cup flour
1/ teaspoon baking powder

1 4.5 oz can chopped green
   chilies, drained
1/2 teaspoon hot sauce
1/3 cup shredded mozzarella
1/3 cup shredded sharp
   cheddar

salsa

Serves 6

Pigeon Peas Accra

A favorite appetizer from the Island of Tobago

Crush peas with fork, add all other ingredients, mix well.

Fry by spoonfuls in hot oil.

Garnish with almost any thing: parsley, chopped hard boiled eggs, sliced black olives, crushed nuts.

Serve hot.

1 cup pigeon peas
   or 1 cup green peas
1 medium onion,
   chopped
2 eggs, beaten
1 stalk celery, chopped
1/2 cup flour
1 teaspoon baking
   powder
1/2 teaspoon salt
1/4 cup liquid from peas

Serves 4

"Cows are my passion."
Dombey and Son
Charles Dickens, 1848

Baked Almond Brie

Purely decadent, creamy and crunchy simultaneously,
this brie deserves to accompany a really good champagne.

Broil almonds in toaster oven or regular oven on baking sheet only until brown and fragrant. Watch carefully so they don't burn.

Heat regular oven to 350"
Place brie on round plate and slice off white crust on top.

Sprinkle toasted almonds liberally on top of cheese.

Turn off oven. Place brie in warm oven and let gently melt until soft but not runny, about 10 minutes.

Put hot plate onto larger plate and surround with sliced apples, pears or crackers.

1- 2 ounce package slivered almonds

1- 15 ounce round brie cheese

Sliced apples, pears or crackers

Serves 10 or more as an appetizer.

Cheese Straws

*A very simple yet delicious appetizer, this is a good one
to make with young help on a rainy day.
Recipe may be doubled.*

Rub butter into flour, add cheese and seasoning. Bind to a stiff paste with the egg yolk and water, Roll out thinly and cut into straws. Bake in a 375° oven for about 5 to 7 minutes.

Serve hot.

4 Tablespoons flour
4 Tablespoons butter
4 Tablespoons grated cheese
(any kind will do but hard cheeses seem to work best)
about 1/2 an egg yolk.
salt & pepper
a little water

Makes appetizers for about four.

Corn Fritters

Serve as a prelude to a Southern style dinner
or as a side dish with a bean chili.

Sift flour, baking powder and salt together.

Beat eggs until fluffy.

Add beaten eggs, pepper and melted butter to dry ingredients and beat with a fork until smooth.

Stir in creamed corn. (Batter should be of a dropping consistency. Add a bit of milk if it needs thinning.)

Drop by spoonfuls into preheated oil (375°) in a large frying pan

Fry for 4 or 5 minutes or until evenly browned. Serve hot by themselves or with a dip of your choosing.

1 1/2 cups flour
2 teaspoons baking powder
1/2 teaspoons salt
1/4 teaspoons pepper
2 eggs
1 Tablespoon melted butter
1 -1/2 cups creamed corn

Chili Cheese Dip

You can make this ahead and refrigerate overnight for a "pop-it-in-the-oven easy" appetizer.

On the bottom of a 9" x 13" pan spread the cream cheese. Layer the chili on top of it; Place the diced green chiles on top of the chili. Top with the grated cheddar.

May be refrigerated for later use.

Before serving, place in a 350^0 oven and bake for 30 minutes. During the last 5 minutes of baking, add garnishes and return to oven. Serve it right away with a basket of tortilla chips and a cold Mexican beer. For more than 6 people you might want to make 2, because the first one will go faster than Poncho Villa at a taco-eating contest.

2 - 16 ounce packages of cream cheese, softened
2 - 12 ounce cans vegetarian chili, or make your own.
1 small can diced green chilies
2 cups grated cheddar

Sliced black olives and green onions for garnish

Tortilla chips

Soups

Soup is the path to everyone's heart.

"Oliver Twist has asked for more!"
Charles Dickens, 1837

Split Pea Soup
Thick as Fog!

Our simple, healthy version created by Ray Dunn is vegetarian and low-fat. We garnish it with our own homemade croutons.

Lightly saute in a little butter	1 cup finely diced yellow onion
Bring to a boil. Cook covered on simmer for 1 to 1 1/2 hours or until carrots are done.	5 cups water 1 pound green split peas (rinsed) 1 medium carrot, diced salt & pepper to taste
Thin with water	

Serves 6-8
Garnish with Colophon Croutons.

Colophon Croutons

Use as a garnish for soups or salads.

Cube enough day-old bread to cover a cookie sheet.
Put the bread cubes in a large bowl.
Mix together:
1/2 cup melted butter
1 teaspoon each of garlic, thyme, parsley and tarragon

Drizzle butter mixture over bread, stiring cubes around.
Spread evenly onto cookie sheet.
Bake at 400^{0} for 8 minutes. Stir well. Put back in oven until toasty brown. Cool before serving.

Gazpacho

A spicy, cold tomato soup full of healthy veggies.
Excellent for a summer meal.

Mix together in a large bowl the day before serving and chill overnight.

3 -15 ounce cans diced tomatoes or fresh tomatoes that have been peeled and chopped
46 ounce vegetable juice cocktail
1/4 cup chopped white onion
3 cucumbers, peeled, seeded, diced
1/2 bunch celery, diced
1/4 bunch cilantro, minced
1 bunch green onions, chopped
2 Tablespoons olive oil
2 Tablespoons minced garlic
A good dash Tabasco
1 teaspoon salt
1 teaspoon pepper

Thin with chilled vegetable juice if too thick.
Chill pot and bowls in freezer before serving.
For variety add a dollop of sour cream on top.

Garnish with Tortilla Chips

Serves 8-10

Mexican Corn and Bean Sopa

One of the most popular soups ever to come from the Colophon, the Mexican Corn & Bean Sopa has been featured in many publications since we created it. It's low in fat and delicious. We've made it fast to prepare, too.

Saute in a little olive oil	1 medium finely diced onion 3 cloves minced garlic
Add to soup pot and heat to a slow boil	1-15 ounce can diced tomatoes (or equal amount of chopped fresh tomatoes and tomato juice. 2- 15 ounce can red kidney beans (drained) 1- 24 ounce can vegetable juice
Mix spices in a small bowl, then add hot water to a paste-like consistency, Add to pot and heat	3 teaspoons chili powder 1 teaspoon sugar 1 teaspoon cumin 1/2 teaspoon black pepper
Add to pot; heat to 160° Simmer for 1 to 2 hours.	1 lb bag of frozen corn kernals

Thin with water or vegetable juice

**Garnish with blue and yellow Tortilla Chips
Serves 6-8**

*"And it never mattered how cold it was, or how much
it snowed, because Mama Bear always had something
hot on the stove to keep them warm."*
Mama Colophon's Bedtime Stories

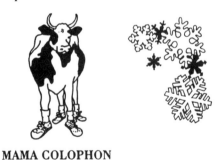

MAMA COLOPHON
(our founder)

Spicy Thai Rice Soup

*A wonderful peanut rice soup flavored with
spicy ginger root, onions and peppers.*

Combine in soup pot cook 20 minutes	1-1/4 cups rice 3 cups water
Chop remaining ingredients in food processor then add to soup pot.	2 carrots 2 ounces ginger root 1 medium onion 1 bell pepper 3 cloves garlic 1 teaspoon cumin 2 teaspoon curry 1 teaspoon black pepper
Heat to a slow boil thin with 2 cups water, and simmer for 30 minutes or longer	1 teaspoon salt a dash of cayenne pepper 4 ounces peanut butter

Garnish with peanuts

Serves 4-6

"The natives took a big black pot they'd gotten from a whaling vessel, had the suprised missionaries for dinner, and decided shortly after that eating vegetarian tasted a whole lot better."
Mama Colophon's Bedtime Stories

Almond Bean Soup

Cover the beans in water and soak over night.

Drain the beans and cook them in the vegetable broth until tender.

Crush almonds in a blender or pound them to pieces. Stir the almonds into the beans.

Add the leeks, garlic, sugar and wine. Cook 10 more minutes, then put through a strainer or serve as is.

Garnish with 1 tablespoon of sour cream in each bowl.

1/2 cup navy beans

3 cups vegetable broth

3/4 cups blanched almonds

2 large leeks, finely chopped
1 garlic clove, minced
1 teaspoon sugar
1/2 cup white wine
1/2 cup sour cream
salt and pepper to taste

Serves 4

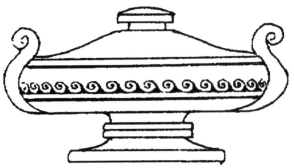

"In Damascus, Popeye won the best soup award with by adding spinach to lentils."
Mama Colophon's Bedtime Stories

MAMA COLOPHON
(our founder)

Syrian Lentil Soup

Wash and clean the lentils. Cover with cold water and cook slowly uncovered until tender.

Wash spinach leaves and break them up into small pieces. Add these and 1 cup of water to the lentils. Continue cooking until the spinach is done, adding more water if necessary.

Heat the olive oil in a skillet and add the onion , garlic, celery and salt, cook until tender and blended. Add this to the lentils. Mix the lemon juice with the flour stir it into the soup.

Cook gently stirring occasionally until the soup is rather thick.

Garnish with a sprinkle of parmesan cheese.

1 1/2 cups dried lentils
2 1/2 pounds spinach
1/4 cup olive oil
3/4 cup onion (chopped)
4 cloves garlic (chopped)
1   stalk celery (chopped)
3/4 cup lemon juice
1 -teaspoon flour
chopped chives

Serves 6

Salads

"*My salad days, when I was green in judgement.*"
Shakespeare, Antony & Cleopatra I v 73

Turkish Cucumber
Salad

Take a trip to Turkey with this great salad

Peel , split and scoop out the seeds of the cukes. Cut in very thin slices or long shreds. Put in a colander, sprinkle with the salt, and let drain for 1 or 2 hours. Then rinse briefly under cold water, drain again and pat dry.

Mix the yogurt with the pepper and lemon juice. Combine with the cucumbers, mint and parsley. Marinate several hours before serving

2 large cucumbers
2 teaspoons salt

1 cup yogurt
1/4 teaspoon freshly
   ground black pepper
1 Tablespoon lemon juice
1 Tablespoon fresh mint
1 Tablespoon chopped
   parsley

MAMA COLOPHON
(our founder)

Serves 4

Finnish Wilted Cucumber Salad

Wilted cucumbers are quite yummy.

Peel , split and scoop out the seeds of the cukes. Cut in very thin slices or long shreds. Put in a colander, sprinkle with the salt, and let drain for 1 or 2 hours. Then rinse briefly under cold water, drain again and pat dry.

Make a sweet and sour dressing with the rest of the ingredients. Pour the dressing over the cucumbers, cover with plastic wrap, and let stand for at least 3 hours before serving, by which time the cukes will have wilted.

2 large cucumbers
2 teaspoons salt

1/2 cup cider vinegar
2 Tablespoons water
3 Tablespoons sugar
1/4 teaspoon freshly
 ground black pepper
2 Tablespoons chopped dill
2 Tablespoons chopped
 parsley

Serves 4

Famous Cucumber Quotes:
"As cold as cucumbers."
Beaumont & Fletcher, 1615
Cupid's Revenge -act I

"But not near as tasty."
Mama Colophon's Bedtime Stories.

"Tis the time of salads."
Laurence Stern
Tristram Shandy, book 1

Orange & Radish Salad

Put lemon juice in a bowl and stir in the sugar and salt until completly dissolved.

1/3 cup lemon juice
2 Tablespoons sugar
1/4 teaspoon sugar

Using a sharp knife, cut off the peel and pithy part of the oranges, and slice them into bite size sections. Wash the radishes, trim off the tops and grate coarsely.

4 large navel oranges
1 bunch red radishes

Combine the oranges and radishes in a salad bowl, pour the lemon mixture over them and mix gently. Refrigerate until chilled. Serve very cold.

Serves 4

Green Bean & Tomato Salad

Prepare the dressing 2 or more hours before serving. Put all ingredients, except the oil, in a jar or cruet with lid, and shake to dissolve the salt, sugar and mustard. Add the oil and shake again.

Trim the beans and cut into 1-inch pieces. Drop them into a pot of rapidly boiling salted water. Boil uncovered, until just tender to the bite, about 5 to 7 minutes from the time the water returns to a rolling boil. Drain and run cold water over the beans, then dry thoroughly.
Remove the garlic and shake dressing just before adding. Toss with the salad. Cover and refrigerate 3 to 4 hours.

Dressing:
2 cloves garlic peeled and cut in half
1/2 teaspoon sugar
1/8 teaspoon dry mustard
1/8 teaspoon oregano
1 Tablespoon grated onion
1 Tablespoon lemon juice
2 Tablespoon red wine vinegar
1/4 cup olive oil

Salad:
1 pound green beans
3 Tablespoons green onion finely chopped
2 Tablespoons Blue cheese crumbled
3 ripe tomatoes sliced thin
Lettuce leaves

Green Bean & Tomato Salad
(continued)

To Serve:
Line salad plates with lettuce leaves.
Top with a ring of overlapping tomato slices. Spoon a mound of the bean salad onto the center of the tomato slices.

Garnish with the egg slices, pimientos and olives.

Garnish:
2 hard boiled eggs, sliced
2 ounce jar sliced pimientos, drained

12 ripe black olives

Serves 4

"I came, I saw, I conquered."
Julius Caesar, 100-44 B.C.

MAMA COLOPHON
(our founder)

"I came, I saw, I ate"
Mama Colophon's Bedtime Stories

The Best Avocado
Caesar Salad

No eggs needed in this one. We like it with heavy garlic, so use less if you don't want to taste it all day. Also, many people put the dressing in the bowl first and then add the lettuce. That's fine if you want most of the dressing to stay in the bowl. We prefer to drizzle over the top, then toss.

Prep lettuce into big bowl.

Salad:
2 large heads of green leaf or romaine lettuce, washed throughly, dried and torn into bite size bits.

Mix dressing ingredients together in cruet with lid and shake until blended. May be done hours ahead and held in refrigerator.

Dressing:
1/3 cup olive oil
6 garlic cloves, pressed or minced
3 teaspoons lemon juice
1 teaspoon Worcestershire sauce
Freshly ground pepper to taste

1 cup shredded parmesan cheese

Drizzle dressing over lettuce in bowl. Toss together with parmesan. Garnish top of salad with avocado slices and croutons if you wish.

2 or 3 peeled, sliced ripe avocados
Croutons

Serve with French bread.

Serves 6

Potato Cheese Salad

This tasty salad is great in the summertime, Chill well in advance and take it out for a picnic or a sunset cruise

Peel dice and boil potatoes until nearly fork tender.

Drain water and mix in cheese gently.

Cut up egg and add with other ingredients to the potato mixture.

Chill well before serving

4 medium potatoes
2 Tablespoons mayonnaise
2 Tablespoons yellow mustard
2 Tablespoon green pepper
2 Tablespoons red pepper
   (both finely chopped)
3 green onions, chopped
1/2 cup grated cheddar
1 hard boiled egg

Serves 6

Wow, Captain Columbus, this salad is so good! Did you make it?

Chilled Vegetable Pasta Salad

A cold pasta salad to make the day before.

Cook spaghetti and drain.

6 ounces spaghetti noodles

Combine oil, vinegar and spices in cruet with lid and shake. Pour over warm spaghetti. Cool in refrigerator.

1/3 cup vegetable oil
1/4 cup cider vinegar
1/2 teaspoon basil
1/4 teaspoon black pepper

Toss vegetables in cool spaghetti and chill throughly before serving.

3/4 cup chopped tomato
1/2 cup chopped celery
1/2 cup chopped cucumber
1/3 cup chopped green onion
1/4 cup chopped fresh parsley

Garnish with tomato wedges and parmesan to taste.

tomato wedges

parmesan cheese

Serves 6

Serves 6 as a main course

Side
Dishes

Spicy Peanut Sauce

*Though traditionally used for Chicken Satay, our favorite
Thai sauce can accompany raw vegetables or the vegetable
potstickers on the next page.*

Gently melt peanut butter in bottom of saucepan.

1/2 cup smooth peanut butter

Add all other ingredients.

1/2 Tablespoon chili powder
3 garlic cloves, pressed or chopped

Heat on medium-high until thick, stirring often.

1 1/4 cup coconut milk
1/4 cup soy sauce
1 Tablespoon lime juice

**Makes about two cups
of sauce.**

Vegetarian Potstickers

These may be filled with nearly anything from the garden.

Heat 2 Tablespoons oil in saute pan at medium heat.

Stir fry all vegetables until softened.

In a bowl, combine garlic and vinegar with cooked vegetables.

Lay wonton wrappers on towel and place small amounts of vegetables in center of each. Wet edges of wrappers with water and crimp seams together tightly.

Reheat saute pan at medium. Coat pan with olive oil. Cook potstickers until browned. Add water and soy sauce and cover. Steam about 2 minutes. Remove and drain excess moisture off.

Potstickers are slippery. Serve them on separate plates for each guest. Chopsticks are good implements for those who can use them.

2 Tablespoons olive oil

1 medium zucchini diced
1 red bell pepper diced
1 med red onion peeled and diced
3 medium carrots diced

2 cloves minced garlic
2 Tablespoons balsamic vinegar

1 package won ton wrappers
small bowl water

1 cup water
1/4 cup soy sauce
1/4 cup olive oil

Serves 8-10 as a side dish or appetizer.
Great served dipped in peanut sauce.

Hawaiian Rice

Take a trip to the islands!
May be served with vegetables stir fried in terriaki sauce

Prepare rice according to package instructions, adding pineapple juice in place of part of the water.

1 cup Jasmati rice
1 cup water
1 cup pineapple juice
1 Tablespoon butter
dash salt

When rice is cooked and water absorbed, stir in pineapple chunks.

1 cup pineapple chunks
1 cup macadamia nuts

Pour rice onto platter and garnish with macadamia nuts.

Makes about 5 cups of rice.

Cinnamon Rice

Sinfully delicious.

Melt two tablespoons butter in deep sauce pan over medium heat.

4 Tablespoons butter

Reduce heat, add carrots, celery and onion and cook covered for 10 minutes. Stir occasionally.

1/2 cup diced carrots
1/2 cup diced celery
1/2 cup diced white onion

Add rice, salt, cinnamon, and water to pan and bring to a boil over high heat. When the water has reduced to the level of the rice, lower heat, cover and cook 15 to 20 minutes, stirring occasionally. Just prior to serving, add remaining butter.

2 cups long grain rice
1/2 teaspoon salt
1 Tablespoon ground cinnamon
1/2 cup golden raisins
6 cups water

Makes about 8 cups of rice.

Hummus

*An exotic blend of healthy stuff that tastes great on bagels,
as a vegetable dip, or on cucumber sandwiches.*

Puree in food
processor for 3 to
4 minutes.

4 cups cooked, drained
garbonzo beans
2 teaspoons cumin
2 teaspoons salt
1/2 cup minced garlic
1 cup olive oil

Add

1-15 oz can or jar of Tahini
(ground sesame seeds)
1 3/4 cups lemon juice

Blend in food
processor or mixer
until thoroughly
blended, then
refrigerate.

Makes approximately 4 cups

44

Spinach in Sour Cream

What a yummy thing to do with spinach.

Carefully wash and stem the spinach leaves. Throw them into a pot of boiling water and boil no longer than 3 minutes.

Remove from pot and drain well. Melt butter in heavy pan. Add the flour, blend well.

Add spinach, onion, sour cream, salt and pepper. Heat thoroughly and serve immediately.

3 pounds young tender spinach

2 Tablespoons butter
1 Tablespoons flour

1 Tablespoons minced onion
1/4 cup thick sour cream
salt & pepper

Serves 6-8

Spicy Oven Fries

Less greasy than deep fried and tastes even better.

Preheat oven to 400°

Scrub potatoes and slice lengthwise into 8ths. Make small cuts across top of fries. In bowl, combine 6 tablespoons melted butter, garlic and hot sauce.

6 medium russet potatoes

1/4 pound butter or margarine, melted
2 cloves pressed garlic
1/2 teaspoon. hot sauce
cayenne pepper to taste

Toss potato spears in bowl with butter mixture and cayenne pepper until coated.

Place on baking sheet. Bake 30 minutes, or until done, basting once with any remaining butter mixture.

6-8 Servings

Coconut Milk
Garlic Mashed Potatoes

The best potatoes for this are yellow Finn or Yukon gold.

Put potatoes in a pot with enough water to cover, boil until fork tender. Drain well.

Combine all ingredients in a food processor or mixing bowl until smooth.

Garnish with some parsley or a big dab of melting butter on top.

6 medium potatoes,
   (peeled & quartered)
1 cup milk
1/4 cup coconut milk
3 Tablespoons butter
3 cloves garlic
   (finely minced)
1 teaspoon salt
1/2 teaspoon pepper

8 Servings

"*The coach became a pumpkin and the steeds turned back into mice, but Cinderella caught her prince despite it all. And they all went into therapy together.*"

Mama Colophon's Bedtime Stories

MAMA COLOPHON
(our founder)

Pumpkin Blueberry Corn Bread

A Fall treat for Thanksgiving or any other time

Preheat Oven to 350°
Spray 8" loaf pan with vegetable spray

Mix all ingredients except blueberries together in food processor or mixer until thoroughly blended. Fold blueberries gently into mixture

Bake 50 minutes or until center is done

3/4 cup whole wheat flour
1 teaspoon baking powder
1/2 teaspoon baking soda
1/2 teaspoon nutmeg
1/2 teaspoon cloves
1/2 teaspoon cinnamon
1/4 teaspoon salt
1/2 cup yellow corn meal
1/4 cup butter, softened
1/3 cup brown sugar
2 eggs
1/2 cup pumpkin puree
1/2 cup milk
1/2 cup blueberrries

Serve with Honey Rum Butter
Makes 1 loaf

Honey Rum Butter

Blend all ingredients and refrigerate.

Makes about 1/2 Cup

1 stick of butter
1 Tablespoon rum
1 Tablespoon honey
dash grated orange rind

(For Orange Butter, substitute Grand Marnier for the rum!)

Colophon Manager Dave Killian's grandfather grew the largest zucchini in the State of Washington in the 1970s. He has a special affinity for the vegetable.

Oregon Zucchini Cashew Bread

The poor zucchini, so popular, yet everyone wants to give you one, or two, or an entire box full.

Preheat oven to 350°.
Spray two 8″ loaf pans with vegetable spray
Blend ingredients thoroughly in mixing bowl or food processor.

3 eggs
1 cup canola oil
2 cups sugar or honey
2 cups grated zucchini
2 teaspoons vanilla

Sitr together dry ingredients in separate bowl and combine with first ingredients until blended.

1 teaspoon baking soda
3 cups flour
1/4 teaspoons baking powder
1 teaspoon salt
2 teaspoons cinnamon
1 teaspoons nutmeg

Stir in cashews.

1 cup cashews

Bake 50 minutes or until center is done

Makes 2 loaves

51

Herbed Tomato
Barbecue Sauce

*The easy alternative to buying those bottled sauces that
never quite taste the way you wish they would.
Brush on vegetable skewers or use as a dipping sauce.*

Stir all ingredients into
large sauce pan.
Bring to a boil, stirring
occasionally to prevent
burning.

Reduce heat and
simmer 30 minutes.

Cool, place in covered
containers and
refrigerate throughly.

2-15 ounce cans tomato sauce
    w/bits
2 cups finely chopped sweet or
    yellow onion
1 cup dry red wine
3/4 cup dark corn syrup
5 cloves garlic, pressed or minced
2 teaspoons crushed dried basil
1 1/2 teaspoons thyme
1 teaspoon hot pepper sauce

Makes about 6 cups

Barbecued Vegetable Skewers

Prep this ahead of time and you'll have time to visit with guests instead of cooking.

Cut vegetables into large chunks, at least 2 inches square.

Arrange on metal skewers, alternating for color.

Place on hot barbecue grill and brush with sauce.

Cook 10 minutes and turn each skewer.

Cook 5-10 more minutes and serve hot.

2 large onions
1 green bell pepper
1 red bell pepper
1 medium zucchini,
    cut in half,
        seeds removed
10 mushrooms

Makes 4-6 skewers

Entrees

"Quiche me, you fool! thought Sleeping Beauty as she lay helplessly waiting for the handsome, but totally inept prince to get up the nerve to do it. I'll be stuck here forever, she moaned silently."

Mama Colophon's Bedtime Stories

Quick Broccoli Cheddar Quiche

This is great brunch food! Serve with fresh fruit and little muffins and you've got it. Leftovers save well and are microwavable.

Pre-heat oven to 375°.
Sprinkle flour in the bottom of a glass pie pan.
Place pie crust in pan.

1 Tablespoon flour
One pre-made refrigerator pie crust at room temperature

Place in pie crust

1 cup chopped broccoli
1 cup grated cheddar cheese
1 cup grated mozzarella cheese

Beat together gently and pour over broccoli cheese mixture.

3 large eggs
1 1/2 cups 2% milk
1 Tablespoon cornstarch
1 teaspoon cayenne pepper
1 teaspoon hot dry mustard

Bake 40-50 minutes or until center is no longer liquid. Cool 15 minutes before serving.

Serves 6

Broccoli Cheddar Pot Pie

A rich and creamy pot pie with a parmesan biscuit topping.
Great winter day food!

Preheat oven to 350.⁰
Microwave ingredients on high until potatoes are soft;
place into large bowl:

Microwave milk and cheese for 3 minutes, or until they can be blended together. Pour mixture over the vegetables

Add to vegetable mixture and mix thoroughly.
Scoop 1 1/2 cups of mixture into oven proof soup bowls. Top with parmesan biscuit rounds (recipe on next page). Brush with egg white.

1/2 cup butter
1 lg onion, chopped
2 carrots, peeled & diced
3 celery stalks, sliced
2 large potatoes
    cut in small cubes
1/4 cup sherry
2 Tablespoons minced garlic

3 cups milk
1 cup grated cheddar or
    processed cheese spread

50 oz canned cream of potato
    soup
1 cup cheddar cheese shredded
3 cups chopped broccoli
    (if using frozen, thaw first)
1/4 tsp white pepper
1/3 Tablespoon garlic powder

Bake for 20-25 minutes until bubbly and golden brown
Makes 6 large pot pies

Pot Pie Parmesan
Biscuit Topping

Preheat oven 350°.
Mix ingredients
on slow speed of
mixer just until
blended

2 cups flour
1 Tablespoon baking powder
1 teaspoon sugar
1/2 teaspoon salt
1/2 teaspoon pepper
1/2 teaspoon paprika
1/2 cup parmesan shredded
2 Tablespoons chopped
  green onions

Add butter pieces
and mix until coarse.
Blend in milk.

1/3 cup unsalted butter cut
into 1/2 inch pieces
3/4 cup milk

Turn out onto a floured board and knead until the dough
is no longer too sticky to work with.
Roll out dough to 1/4" thick .
Cut dough with paring knife, tracing around top of an
upside down soup bowl.-Place biscuit rounds on the filled
bowls.-Brush tops with egg whites .
Bake for 20-25 minutes until pot pies are bubbly and
golden brown.

Makes 6 large pot pie toppings

Chili Relleno

Anaheim chili peppers have a delicate skin, therefore, when you peel the roasted peppers try not to tear up the flesh of the pepper, and don't worry about getting all the skin off.

Preheat broiler and roast chiles until blistered, about 5 minutes on each side.

Drain tofu and let sit for 5 to 10 minutes in a bowl. Drain again to remove excess water. Add garlic, salt, parsley, green onions and cheese. Blend in a mixer until creamy.

Mix baking soda with flour and whisk in soda water and 1/2 teaspoon salt until batter is thick and creamy.

Place peppers in a bowl or brown paper bag until cool enough to handle. Carefully peel off outer layer of charred skin and slice chili along the length of one side to remove seeds. Try to keep stems and pods intact if possible. Spoon some of the tofu filling and beans into each chili pod.

Heat 1/2 inch of oil in a large frying pan. Dip each chili in the batter until well coated. Fry in hot oil until golden brown (2-3 min. each side. Serve hot topped with the sauce of your choice.

10 fresh Anaheim chiles
1 pound. firm tofu
5 garlic cloves
2 teaspoon salt
1 cup parsley, chopped
1 bunch green onions, minced
1 cup grated jack cheese
1/2 cup flour
1/2 teaspoon baking soda
1 - 10 ounce bottle of soda water
1/2 teaspoon salt
1 1/2 cups refried black beans
1 cup corn oil

Serves 6

60

Sweet Onion
Enchiladas

Prepare before a party and pull it out of the oven as every-one arrives. Great with salsa and sour cream on the side.

Preheat oven to 350°.

In bottom of 9" x 13" glass baking dish, spread 1/2 can hot enchilada sauce.

Warm other half can enchilada sauce in skillet. Using tongs, warm tortilla in sauce briefly on each side until soft but not falling apart and place gently in baking dish.

Fill with spoonfuls of cheese and onion, roll up, push toward the end of pan and repeat.

When baking dish is full, cover enchiladas with remaining can of mild enchilada sauce and jack cheese. Bake 20-30 minutes, or until bubbly.

1 can hot enchilada sauce
1 can mild enchilada sauce

2 cups grated jack cheese
1 cup grated cheddar cheese
1 cup chopped Walla Walla
  or other sweet onions

8 large corn tortillas

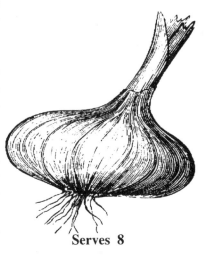

Serves 8

Jamaican
Red Beans & Rice

A traditional, wonderful Jamaican dish.
Discovered on another one of Ray's exotic sailing trips.

In a sauce pan add coconut milk and water to the beans and rice, cover, bring to a boil and turn down to a simmer.

2 cups canned coconut milk
4 cups water
3 cups white rice
1 cup red beans

Cook until beans are tender. 1 to 1 1/2 hours

Add coconut, garlic, thyme chives and cloves, and simmer for another 30 minutes adding more water if it gets too thick.

1/4 cup dried coconut, grated
3 cloves garlic, minced
1 teaspoon thyme
3 Tablespoons chives, chopped
4 whole cloves

Serves 6

Spanakopita

Contributed by Teresa Brainard,
waitstaff manager and fabulous cook!

Preheat oven to 375°.
Saute onion and garlic in butter until lightly browned. Add spinach. Cook uncovered until tender and no liquid remains in pan.

1 Tablespoon butter
1 small onion, diced
2 cloves garlic, crushed

2 lbs fresh spinach

Add nutmeg, salt and pepper, let cool.

1/8 teaspoon nutmeg
salt & pepper to taste

Combine feta, egg, egg yolk and cream. Chop spinach mixture coarsely and stir into the egg mixture. Lay 1 sheet filo dough on flat surface, brush lightly with melted butter. Layer remaining 7 sheets over the first, brushing each layer lightly with the melted butter.

1 cup feta cheese, crumbled
1 egg plus 1 egg yolk
3 Tablespoons cream

1/2 cup melted butter
8 sheets filo dough

Spoon spinach mixture down long edge of filo dough. Fold up covering mixture, folding sides over about 1 inch. Roll up tightly, brush roll with butter. Place seam side down on baking sheet. Bake 20 to 25 minutes until golden brown, serve warm

Serves 6

Black Bean Taquitos con Guacamole

These are great hot, cold or any where in between

In a small frying pan heat oil until a drop of water sizzles when placed in it. Put a tortilla in, frying lightly on both sides. Fry just enough so that it is still pliable but not at all crisp. Remove from the pan to a paper towel and blot off any excess oil.

Gently combine all ingredients for the black bean filling. Put a small amount of the filling on one end of the tortilla. Roll it up and hold it together with one of the toothpicks. Place it in a baking dish and put in oven on low. Repeat process until all the Taquitos are in the oven.

Serve on a bed of lettuce. Top with chunky guacamole and crumbled cheese. Serve salsa on the side.

12 corn tortillas
1/2 cup corn oil

Black bean filling
1 cup cooked black beans
2 Tablespoons minced onion
1 teaspoon ground cumin
2 teaspoon chili powder
1 small tomato , chopped fine
12 wooden tooth picks

Garnish
1 cup shredded lettuce
1 cup guacamole
1 cup feta cheese
1 cup salsa

Serves 6

Chunky Guacamole

Gently mix all ingredients in bowl with fork.

If you are not serving the guacamole right away cover tightly with clear wrap, pushing the wrap lightly onto the mixture to keep it from turning dark, then refrigerate until used.

2 large avocados peeled and chopped
1/2 large white, sweet onion, chopped
1/2 teaspoon cumin
1 teaspoon chili powder
Dash garlic salt
1 Tablespoon lemon juice

Serves 6

Asian Noodle Salad

Fast and yummy.

Combine in large bowl

1 Tablespoon sugar
3 Tablespoons lime juice
3 Tablespoons water
3 Tablespoons soy sauce
2 Tablespoons creamy
    peanut butter
4 crushed garlic cloves

Boil noodles according to
directions on box.

6 ounces uncooked
    spaghetti noodles

Toss hot noodles with peanut sauce. Add sprouts,
green onions and peanuts.

1/2 cups bean sprouts
1/3 cup sliced
    green onions
1 cup dry roasted,
    unsalted peanuts

Serve warm in large bowls
with chopsticks.

Serves 2

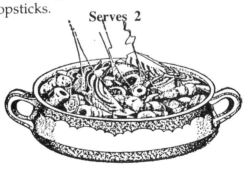

Mushroom Casserole

A quick and easy cold weather delight for mushroom lovers. Try it with different kinds of mushrooms, porto bellos are my favorite, but shitakes are also grand.

Preheat oven to 450.°
Cream seasonings thoroughly into butter.
Spread a part of this butter mixture on the bottom of a casserole dish, arrange on mixture the mushroom caps, open side up. Dot each cap with some of the remaining butter mixture until all is used. Add the cream, salt and pepper. Bake for 10 minutes. Serve at once.

1/3 cup butter
1 teaspoon parsley, minced
1 teaspoon chives, minced
1 teaspoon onion juice
1 teaspoon salt
1/4 teaspoon cayenne pepper
1 teaspoon nutmeg
1/2 teaspoon tarragon
1 cup cream
salt & pepper to taste
18 large mushrooms
(washed and stemmed)

Serves 6

Desserts

Kinda like Mom made.

"In the spring a young man's fancy lightly turns to thoughts of love..."
Alfred Lord Tennyson, 1809-1892

"...and thoughts of pie."
Mama Colophon's Bedtime Stories

MAMA COLOPHON
(our founder)

"Kiss till the cows come home",
Beaumont & Fletcher, 1616
The Scornful Lady, act III

70

Finnish Apple Pie

Taimi's grandparents came from Finland and her grandma was a cook, so she tends to collect recipes from the far north. This one, fortunately, does not contain fish heads or any of the stuff Grandma used to use.

Pre-heat oven to 450 .°

Blend cheese into the pie crust dough. Split dough in half and roll out for pie. Place one in pie pan and trim edge, leaving 1/2 inch all around.

Combine sugar and seasonings and toss with apples.

Layer apples into the pie crust and dot with butter. Sprinkle with lemon juice and peel.

Foll out remaining pastry and place on top of pie. Seal and flute edges. Make several slits on top.

Bake 10 minutes at 450,°
then reduce heat to 375 °
and bake one hour longer until crust is golden.

pastry for a 9-inch double crust pie
1 1/2 cups shredded Finnish cheese-(or Swiss will do)

6 medium sized tart apples, peeled and sliced thin
1 peach, peeled and sliced
1 cup brown sugar
1 Tablespoon cinnamon
1 teaspoon allspice
1/4 teaspoon salt
2 Tablespoons soft butter
1 Tablespoon lemon juice
1/2 teaspoon grated lemon peel

Serves 6

71

Peach Oat Crisp

A fragrant dessert to serve hot out of the oven.

Preheat oven to 375°.

Put two tablespoons butter in bottom of 9"x 13" pan. Place in oven until butter melts. Pull from oven and spread melted butter evenly over bottom of pan.

Arrange peaches in an even layer.

1/2 cup softened butter
3 pounds (6 cups) sliced peaches

In a bowl, combine brown sugar, flour, oats, cinnamon and nutmeg, blend in remaining butter with a fork. Mixture should be crumbly. Sprinkle evenly over peaches, pressing slightly with fork to cover top.

Bake 30-40 minutes or until fruit is tender.

1/2 cup brown sugar
1/2 cup flour
3/4 cup rolled oats
1/2 teaspoon cinnamon
1/2 teaspoon nutmeg

May be topped with whipped cream, vanilla ice cream or served just as it is!

6-8 Servings

Pumpkin Pone

*Pumpkin pone is a favorite confection of
children of all ages in Guyana.*

Preheat oven to 375^0.
Blend pumpkin and coconut together in a medium bowl.
Add cornmeal and blend in margarine.
Add all other ingredients, and mix well. It should be a soft dripping consistency.

Pour into a greased 9"x12" baking pan. The mixture should be 1 to 1 1/2" thick.

Bake uncovered about 20 to 25 minutes or until crisp and brown.
Cut into 2" squares. May be served warm or cool.

1 pound pumpkin, grated
1/2 pound dried coconut, grated
1 cup cornmeal
2 oz. margarine
1/4 cup sugar
1 cup water
1/2 teaspoon cinnamon
1/4 teaspoon grated nutmeg
1/2 teaspoon vanilla extract
dash of salt

Dave's Breakfast
Cookies

Low-fat cookies created by Colophon Chef Dave Killian.
These make great tasting healthy snacks.

Preheat oven to 325°. Mix together in mixing bowl	1 1/2 cups applesauce 1 1/8 cups brown sugar 1/2 cup apple juice 1/6 cup orange juice 1/6 cup lemon juice 2 Tablespoons vanilla
Mix in	1 mashed banana
Stir in	3/4 cup flour 1/2 cup wheat flour 1 Tablespoon baking soda 1/2 Tablespoon cinnamon 1/2 Tablespoon nutmeg 1/2 Tablespon ginger 3/4 teaspoon cloves
Stir in	4 cups oats 2 cups rice crispies 3/4 cup crushed corn flakes 3/4 cup dried fruit

These cookies are very moist. It is easiest to use an ice cream scoop and drop the dough on a parchment lined cookie sheet. Dip fingers into water and pat cookies into flat circles. They will not spread while baking.
Bake for 12-15 minutes.

Makes 24 Cookies

Bapple Cookies

*Like "trail mix" in a cookie, many people eat just these
instead of a full lunch!*

Preheat oven to
350 degrees.
Cream together in
a large bowl

3/4 cup butter
3/4 cup white sugar
1/2 cup brown sugar
3 eggs, added one at a time

Add

3/4 teaspoons vanilla
1/2 cup apple juice
1/8 cup cooled espresso or
  very strong coffee

Mix
together

2 1/2 cups flour
2 teaspoons baking soda
1/2 teaspoon salt
1/2 teaspoon allspice
1/2 teaspoon nutmeg
2 teaspoons cinnamon
3 3/4 cups oats

Stir in and mix
well, scraping sides
and bottom of bowl

1 medium chopped apple
3/4 cup raisins
3/4 cup chocolate chips
1/2 cup chopped walnuts

Drop rounded spoonfuls of dough onto parchment
lined cookie sheet.
Dip fingers into cold water and press cookies into
round, flat patties. (They will not spread while
baking.)
Sprinkle each with 1/2 teaspoon chopped walnuts.
Bake 10-12 min or until light to med brown.
Do not overcook.

Makes about 2 dozen large cookies

Colophon Peanut Butter Pie

*This pie is so delicious, "Bon Appetit"magazine requested
our recipe and printed it in the August 1993 issue.
This recipe makes 2 pies.*

Mix together in a large bowl and set aside.	18 oz cream cheese 1 1/2 cups crunchy peanut butter 1 1/2 cups brown sugar 1 teaspoon vanilla
Whip on low speed for two minutes in chilled bowl Add sugar and whip on high speed until peaks form (do NOT overwhip or cream will turn buttery!)	2 cups heavy whipping cream 1/2 cup powdered sugar
Fold the whipped cream mixture into the peanut butter mixture.	

Spoon Mixture into two 8 inch Chocolate Cookie Crusts.
Spread evenly and freeze pies for 3 hours.

Recipe continued on next page...

continued...

Melt in separate
bowl

2 cups melting chocolate (or
semi-sweet chocolate chips)
with 1/2 cup half & half in the
microwave for 30-45 seconds.
Stir until smooth

Carefully spoon half the
chocolate ganache on the
top of each frozen pie.
Spread evenly and quickly
garnish with 1 Tablespoon
chopped peanuts before
the chocolate sets. Chill for
1 hour before cutting. Use
a knife dipped in hot wa-
ter for cutting.

This recipe makes two pies.
They may be frozen for storage.
To thaw, place in refrigerator for several hours.
They will cut more easily if partially frozen.

Chocolate Cookie Crust

For the Colophon Peanut Butter Pie

Combine well by
hand or
food processor

4 1/2 cups finely ground
chocolate cookie crumbs
1/2 cup butter, melted

Divide in half and press into 2 pie tins.
Bake 7-10 min at 350°.

Peanut Butter Chocolate Brownies

An invention by Taimi, these brownies are made in individual muffin cups for easy serving.

Preheat oven to 350°. Spray 2 one-dozen muffin tins with vegetable spray.

Blend ingredients in bowl or food processor.

Fold in flour and baking powder.

Add 1/2 package of chocolate chips to mixture. Spoon dough into muffin molds and bake 25 minutes.

Remove from oven and while still hot, spread remaining chocolate chips over each brownie. Let sit for five minutes and then spread melted chocolate with a knife.

2/3 cup softened butter
1 cup softened peanut butter
1 1/4 cups sugar
1 1/4 cups brown sugar
1 teaspoon vanilla
3 eggs
8 ounces sour cream

2 cups unsifted flour
2 1/2 tsp baking powder

1 16 ounce package chocolate chips

1 12 ounce package peanut butter chips

Garnish top of each brownie with peanut butter chips. Cool brownies overnight before removing from pan.

Makes 24 Brownies

Mom's Jamocha Rum Cake

*Taimi's busy Mom likes things that are fast to make.
This cake tastes like it took much more work than it did
and it's one of the best you'll ever have.*

Spray 9"X13"pan with vegetable spray.

Prepare cake mix as noted on the box. Mix in instant coffee, pour batter in pan and bake until done.

In saucepan, combine water, sugar, butter and rum. Heat until sugar disolves and butter is melted.

Make small cuts across top of cake with sharp knife. Spoon sauce over hot cake just out of oven.

Cool cake before topping. In chilled bowl, whip cream, sugar, instant coffee and cocoa together until it peaks. Frost cake, sprinkle with shaved chocolate and chill in refrigerator until served.

Cake
1 package moist devils food cake with pudding
1 Tablespoon instant coffee or espresso

Rum Sauce
1/2 cup water
1/2 cup sugar
2 Tablespoons butter
1/2 cup dark rum

Topping
2 cups whipping cream
3 Tablespoons powdered sugar
1 Tablespoon instant coffee or espresso
1 Tablespoon unsweetened cocoa
Grated or chopped milk chocolate

Makes one cake.
10-12 Pieces

Alphabetical Index

Best Vegetarian
Recipes

MAMA COLOPHON
(our founder)

To order more books, phone
Village Books 1-800-392-BOOK

MAMA COLOPHON
(our founder)